AUSTRALIA THE JOURNEY

Fitzgerald River National Park, Western Australia

Chalahn Falls, Lamington National Park, Queensland

Uluṟu, Uluṟu–Kata Tjuṯa National Park, Northern Territory

THE JOURNEYS...
SEA TO DESERT

Escape 1

Seashore Journey 3

Rainforest Journey 23

Mountain Journey 33

Tropical Journey 45

Desert Journey 53

The Journey 67

CONTENTS

The ancient landscapes and diverse wildlife of Australia are a source of endless inspiration to the mind and spirit. This is a land of no half measures. Deep greens to burnt reds, majestic snowy peaks to lush rainforest and inviting beaches, underwater dreamworlds to shimmering billabongs—the embrace of Australia holds them all. Through these images and the music these places have inspired, we will share with you the feelings we have come to realise can be expressed by only one word—*escape*!

sandy pollard

Hill Inlet, Whitsunday Island,
Whitsunday National Park, Queensland

1

The Twelve Apostles, Port Campbell National Park, Victoria

Ocean waves pound a rocky shore

From the azure waters of the Great Barrier Reef to the storm-swept shores of south-west Tasmania, across the Great Australian Bight to Cape Leeuwin, up the coast of Western Australia past North West Cape to the rugged bays and inlets of the Kimberley, along the shores of the Territory to the Gulf of Carpentaria, the coasts of Australia offer unimaginable scenic variety. Australians identify with the sea—most live close by it on the coastal strip, and those bred in the interior come to it for respite from the rigours of the Outback.

SEASHORE JOURNEY

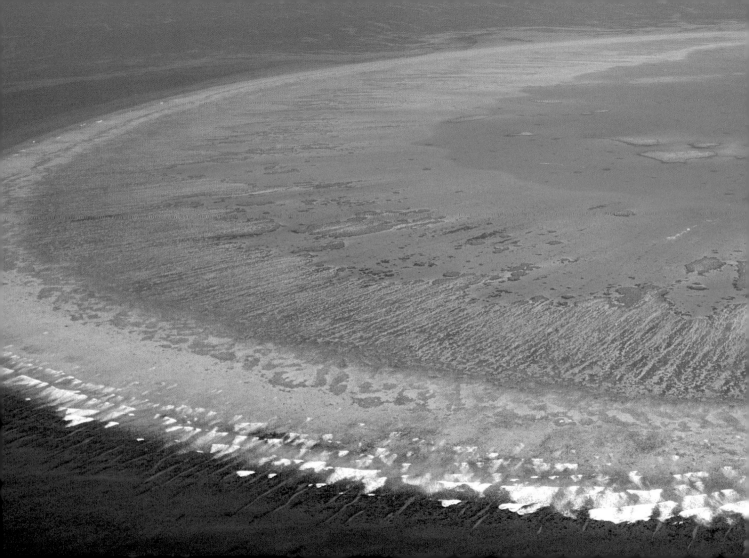

The Great Barrier Reef guards the Queensland coast from the tip of Cape York south to Bundaberg. Truly one of the Earth's wonders, and inscribed on the World Heritage List, the Reef comprises thousands of inner reefs, the outer reefs on the edge of the Continental Shelf, coral cays and atolls, lagoons and fringing reefs around islands. The clear water is sunlit and often placid, inviting scuba divers and snorkellers into its depths to marvel at the myriad jewel-like fish, sea stars, sea cucumbers and corals. Delicate soft corals and anemones wave in the currents; huge rays sway past; sinuous sea-snakes and eels glide from reef overhangs and niches.

Lady Musgrave Island and fringing reef in
the Great Barrier Reef Marine Park

At Cape Tribulation *(left)* in Tropical North
Queensland, the emerald-forested
mountains fall dramatically to the
Coral Sea. This is where the rainforest,
studded with magnificent fan palms
(above), meets the Great Barrier Reef.

7

Studding the Pacific Ocean seven hundred kilometres north-east of Sydney are World Heritage Listed Lord Howe Island *(left)*, Balls Pyramid *(above)* and the Admiralty Islands. Rainforests, mountains, coral reefs and several hundred species of bird exist here in serenity and splendour.

9

The lighthouse on South East Point, Wilsons Promontory, Victoria, built of locally quarried granite in 1859

Breathtaking views over Bass Strait from granite headlands

The southernmost tip of the Australian mainland, Wilsons Promontory is a granite massif jutting into Bass Strait. Sheltered beaches are tucked between the rocky headlands; behind the shore, the forested mountain slopes and valleys are rich in plant and animal life. The pockets of rainforest in the lowlands, such as Lilly Pilly Gully, have special importance as the furthest south warm temperate rainforest in Australia. Open heathland bursts into flower in spring. And the views from the hilltops and headlands are incomparable.

South-west of Melbourne lies Port Campbell National Park. It is reached by the Great Ocean Road, largely cut from the limestone cliffs by soldiers returned from World War I. This coastline sits proudly in the path of the Southern Ocean, defiant limestone stacks jutting forth resisting the pounding waves. Caves, arches and stacks are all sculpted and formed by the Southern Ocean's unremitting power.

Limestone stacks, Port Campbell National Park, Victoria

Just across the narrow Backstairs Passage from South Australia's mainland lies Kangaroo Island. The island's rugged coastline guards the mallee-covered sandy country and eucalypt-clad plateau of the Flinders Chase National Park. Remarkable Rocks *(above)* and Admirals Arch *(left)* have been shaped by the force of the ocean. The island is home to many native birds and animals which thrive because they are not in competition with rabbits and foxes.

15

On the south-west corner of Western Australia lies a majestic and rugged section of coast, thrust out as the continent's last outpost against the fury of the Roaring Forties. The coast is full of contrasts: granite headlands shelter coves like the Salmon Holes *(left)* in Torndirrup National Park; multicoloured cliffs tower over long beaches of white sand; here and there heathlands run down to the beach, grey-green and silver-blue disappearing in a blaze of flowers in springtime.

17

Of such outstanding natural universal values that the area is World Heritage Listed, Shark Bay Marine Park surrounds François Peron National Park on the Peron Peninsula *(left, above)*. Rich in marine life, the Bay is a home of the gentle Dugongs, but is particularly well-known for the Bottlenose Dolphins of Monkey Mia—in this shallow water, wild dolphins come, choosing to interact with humans.

19

Zuytdorp Cliffs, Western Australia

Along the Great Divide are some of Australia's most glorious and important natural environments—the rainforests. Among the giant trees, with their canopies high overhead, and with deep layers of leaf mould underfoot, the silence is deep, broken only by the clear, ringing calls of birds. Lichens and mosses festoon the boles of the trees, fallen logs and boulders in the stream beds; ferns flourish; rivers and creeks flow, spill and jump their way downward. The rainforest is a living laboratory, a profusion of species that is yet to be fully catalogued. Some, like the Southern Cassowary, have their last patches of habitat in these fragile forests.

Rainforest in Dorrigo National Park, New South Wales

23

RAINFOREST JOURNEY

A Crows Nest Fern *(above left)* in the rainforest *(above right)* of Lamington National Park, Queensland

A rainforest stream rushes between moss-covered boulders in Daintree National Park, Queensland

Tchupala Falls, Wooroonooran National Park, Queensland

The Great Dividing Range runs from Cape York, down the east coast to the Atherton Tableland, Mount Warning, the Blue Mountains, the Australian Alps, and then, after the break of Bass Strait, into Tasmania. Through it, along the Australian Heritage Trail, runs a land of pure escape. Low, wind-sculpted alpine trees; harshly cut rocky peaks; glittering snowfields; mighty forests; high grassy meadows; still, calm mountain lakes; thundering waterfalls: all can be explored on a mountain journey.

Arthur Range, Southwest National Park, Tasmania

MOUNTAIN JOURNEY

Cool temperate rainforest in the Ballroom Forest, Cradle Mountain–Lake St Clair National Park, Tasmania

Russell Falls, Mount Field National Park, Tasmania

MacKenzie Falls, the Grampians (Gariwerd) National Park, Victoria

The Grampians (Gariwerd) National Park, Victoria

Mount Kosciuszko, Australia's highest peak, sits in a national park bearing its name. In winter, the snow cover is greater than in Switzerland, and all of New South Wales's skiing grounds are found here. Every year, more and more people visit to experience the exhilaration of swooping down the sparkling slopes, celebrating the joy and excitement of life. In spring and summer, the mountain decks itself with garlands of wildflowers, and travellers come to fish and hike.

Kosciuszko National Park, New South Wales

KOSCIUSZKO

West of Sydney lie the Blue Mountains, named for the delicate haze of blue caused by light striking tiny droplets of oil exuded by the eucalypt forests that clothe the mountain slopes. Here are towering golden cliffs, sparkling waterfalls and mysterious forests that shelter wildlife and many unique plants. The formations in the Jenolan Caves, carved over eons as the Jenolan River dissolved minerals from the limestone of the valley, range from the grandly grotesque to the exquisitely delicate. High above the bustle and industry of Sydney, the climate in the Blue Mountains provides conditions perfect for gardens which enliven the towns with vibrant bursts of colour.

The Three Sisters, the Blue Mountains, New South Wales

A cascade in the Blue Mountains, New South Wales

The escarpment rises over mist-filled valleys of the Blue Mountains, New South Wales

Nature's majesty is never more evident than in Australia's Top End. This is a tropical land of great golden-grey sandstone escarpments over which waterfalls thunder during the Wet; of deep gorges carved by rivers that loop lazily to the sea through vast wetlands that are the haunts of waterbirds, buffalo and crocodiles; of lush rainforest and open woodlands; of billabongs and crystal clear pools. Much of this land is under the guardianship of the traditional owners and galleries of rock art record their culture and their spiritual bond with the land. The Top End offers adventure . . . escape from the humdrum and everyday.

Florence Falls, Litchfield National Park, Northern Territory

TROPICAL JOURNEY

Just east of Katherine, in Nitmiluk National Park, are the thirteen gorges chiselled by the Katherine River into the colourful sandstone of the Arnhem Land Plateau. Deep between looming walls of rock up to 60 metres high, flat-bottomed boats meander through the gorges, while travellers admire the rugged scenery, abundant wildlife and Aboriginal rock art. Boats may reach the fifth gorge, but the only way to explore all thirteen is by canoe. Nitmiluk is breathtaking—the placid nature of the river during the Dry is transformed by rushing sweeps of water during the Wet.

Nitmiluk National Park, Northern Territory

Long before the civilisations of Ancient Egypt, Greece and Rome, people lived in this country of sandstone escarpment and coastal plains. Their creation stories and culture are recorded in pigment on the rocks, and they continue as custodians of the land today. The importance of Kakadu National Park is signified by its World Heritage status. Its beauty and variety are evident in dramatic walls of stone, billabongs and wetlands covered with birds, thundering waterfalls, floodplains and forests. In its estuaries and rivers, the fearsome Saltwater Crocodile and its less aggressive relative, the Freshwater Crocodile, make their home.

Nourlangie Rock and Anbangbang Billabong,
Kakadu National Park, Northern Territory

49

Twin Falls, Kakadu National Park, Northern Territory

The Arnhem Land Escarpment, Kakadu National Park, Northern Territory

PESERT JOURNEY

The desert calls all Australians, even those who have never left the coastal strip. No one can live in this driest continent without being conscious of the vast tracts of red earth, the rocks and dry gullies, the spinifex and dragon lizards, the hardy scrub and rough-hewn ranges that sit over the horizon in the Red Centre. A journey through the Australian desert is an escape to an awesome world of wild beauty, of tough resilient plants and of shy animals that live in this desperately hot land.

The Devil's Marbles, Northern Territory

There may be some unromantic souls who
see Uluṟu as simply a huge block of
sandstone smoothed by eons of
windblown sand. For most, however,
this massive monolith that dominates the
desert is one of the world's natural
wonders. Uluṟu erupts from the plain like
some huge sleeping deity. As the sun
journeys through the blue depths of the
sky, the colours of the great rock change
from palest lavender to flaming red to
deepest crimson.

Uluṟu, Uluṟu–Kata Tjuṯa National Park, Northern Territory

The mighty Flinders Ranges seem to
stretch for ever into the parched Outback,
offering endless adventure to nature lovers
and bushwalkers or to those who simply
enjoy the freedom of wild places.
After spring rains, the slopes are spread
with wildflowers, and, year round, the
mountains shelter such perfectly adapted
creatures as the Yellow-footed Rock-
wallaby that can survive for long periods
without access to water.
By day, the sunlight burnishes
the savage rock with clear, pure colour,
while at night the moonlight gently bathes
the ranges with silver.

Flinders Ranges National Park, South Australia

Throughout Australia's deserts, wildflowers bloom in great profusion after rain has fallen. Each species is in a desperate hurry to set seed so that life will continue after the next Wet, which may be years hence. But, in all the continent, Western Australia's wildflowers are the most beautiful. From the warm and well-watered slopes of the Stirling Ranges to the baking plains surrounding Mt Augustus, riots of wild colours paint the ground with glory.

Wildflowers on the plains around Mt Augustus,
Burringurrah National Park, Western Australia

Scarlet Banksia

Red flowering gum

Red Bottlebrush

Sturt's Desert Pea

The Bungle Bungles *(above)*, Purnululu National Park, the Kimberley, Western Australia, and Wandjina figures *(right)*, spirit people depicted by Kimberley Aborigines

The Kimberley, in the north of Western Australia, is an escaper's dream. Few people venture into its wild and secret places. In the East Kimberley, the extraordinary domes of Purnululu are tiger-striped in bands of orange and grey-green where iron oxide staining the white sandstone is interspersed with bands of lichen. Europeans called them the Bungle Bungles, but their traditional custodians call the area Purnululu. This is a fragile landscape, easily damaged by the passing of travellers. The best and least intrusive view of this eerie moonscape is from the air.

The Lennard River in Windjana Gorge National Park, Western Australia

Boab trees of the Kimberley, Western Australia

Every step taken through this timeless land reminds us that it is at once both beautiful and fragile. The privilege of being able to witness its beauty and feel its power brings also the responsibility to pass this world intact to future generations. All the structures and wealth people create could never be compensation for the loss of our natural heritage. We should perhaps not lose sight of where we come from— to be truly human is to recognise that we are part of nature.

THE JOURNEY

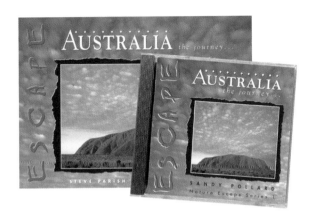

STEVE PARISH MUSIC AUSTRALIA
presents
THE ESCAPE COLLECTION

Australia the Journey • Cry for Wilderness
CDs, Cassettes, Books

Steve Parish, photographer and publisher, and Sandy Pollard, musician, have joined creative forces to produce this brilliant new collection of books and CDs.

Sandy Pollard's exciting and evocative music will lift listeners out of the concerns of the everyday world and transport them deep into wild Australia. This is **Escape Music**.

The brilliant Steve Parish images in the books will enhance and give form to the imaginative journey the music inspires.

DISCOVERY GUIDES, ATLASES AND MAPS

Travel Australia with Steve Parish.
The GUIDES are useful and practical.
There's an ATLAS for any mode of travel
— backpacking, family car or 4WD.
And a MAP for wherever
there's a road or track.

ALL ILLUSTRATED WITH STUNNING STEVE PARISH PHOTOGRAPHS

AN EXTENSIVE RANGE
OF STATE AND REGIONAL MAPS

First published by
Steve Parish Publishing Pty Ltd, 1998
PO Box 1058, Archerfield BC, Qld 4108, Australia
© copyright Steve Parish Publishing Pty Ltd, 1998
ISBN 1 876282 41 X

www.steveparish.com.au

ALL RIGHTS RESERVED.
Photography: Steve Parish
Text: Wynne Webber
Editing, design, art and film production: by
Steve Parish Publishing Pty Ltd, Australia
Printed in Hong Kong by South China Printing